WILD PLACES OF EUROPE

Astounding views of the continent's most beautiful nature sites

———

WOUTER PATTYN

Lannoo

CONTENTS

8	Suðurland — Iceland	130	Lowlands — The Netherlands
30	Indre & Creuse — France	152	Podlaskie — Poland
50	Julijske Alpe — Slovenia	172	Las Extremaduras — Spain
70	Innlandet — Norway	192	Highlands — Scotland
90	Hautes Fagnes — Belgium	212	Heideland — The Netherlands
110	Lapin Maakunta — Finland	232	Finnmark — Norway

PEARLS OF NATURE

When you read this, there's a good chance that I'll be out somewhere on the road, looking for atmospheric landscapes, and searching out rare animals and other wildlife. All of them offered, just like that, by Mother Nature, free for the taking. The list of remarkable locations waiting to be visited is impressive. How or when I want to see them – that's for me to choose. Marvellous! Enchanting!

Truth to tell, I've hardly ever strayed beyond the borders of Europe. There's so much to see here that it seems that I'll never get round to it all. In fact, I've been travelling this alluring continent all my life. I've feasted my eyes, cursed, cried with joy and endlessly enjoyed it. But perhaps what has amazed and astounded me most, is just how brilliant our nature really is. Photographing her, I've come to know her in a very intense way. From almost every trip I return with great stories. Nature experiences of the purest kind that I'm more than happy to share, backed by fine visual material.

Displaying all this beauty in one single book is almost impossible. That is why I've bundled together some of the most beautiful natural pearls for you, a taster if you like, with pictures and stories that will hopefully encourage you to discover superb areas yourself. This book is first and foremost a picture book, the result of infinite patience, endless journeys and masses of perseverance. A book to roam and dream away with, relaxing in your easy chair with photos that will make you want to go out on your own. Not to distant places. Simply, into Europe, on foot, by bike or, like me, in a converted four-wheeler.

Time now perhaps for the distant tropics, Antarctica or other exotic places? No, my journey of discovery through Europe has only just begun. I hope the same for you, that Europe will enthuse you as much as it does me!

Wouter

SUÐURLAND

ICELAND

ICE BIRDS IN THEIR GLITZY TAILOR-MADE SUITS

Here we are, in one of the most beautiful places on this planet. One day's drive to Northern Denmark and three days bobbing on a sea that was far too choppy for my stomach have brought me here. As I carefully drive my van off the boat, I'm overwhelmed with the blissful feeling that this could turn out to be one of the most memorable journeys of my life. An idea intensified by the dense flock of white-tailed eagles circling like a flying door above my head. Not much later, a crying great northern diver gives me goosebumps. If I had to return home now, my trip wouldn't have been wasted. But it's just a start.

Taking the island ring road I end up not far from Höfn on a fairy tale lava beach. As far as the eye can see lie neatly sculpted ice blocks, large and small, apparently very old. Originating from the nearby glacier, after a short passage through the famed Jökulsárlón glacier lagoon, they're dropped onto the beach by tumultuous waves. What a surreal landscape!

I continue my adventure, effortlessly stringing together top locations, from swirling waterfalls to bizarre crater landscapes, as if I had set foot on the moon. And what a stark contrast to the white, icy world I braved here in winter many years ago! This time, in early summer, I've left my woollen socks at home. I'm looking for *Einzelgängers* like the golden plover and the arctic skua, while the mixed bag of other birds on the towering coastal cliffs are also on the program. When all's said and done, birdwatching and photographing is hipper than hip. And now, with summer just around the corner, this part of Iceland is the place to indulge yourself. All animals are now in top condition, having just exchanged their old plumage for flashy tailored suits, ready for the ultimate photo. Some males are clearly out a-wooing, singing their hearts out as they dart excitably back and forth like unguided projectiles, as the females watch with visible pleasure. Passion is in the air here!

Velkomin til Íslands!

FEATURED

Skógafoss. A waterfall high on the bucket list of anyone heading to southern Iceland. Quite rightly so: this is simply a beautiful piece of land art. From a 60 metre-high cliff, a swirling body of water plunges majestically into the abyss. Northern fulmars breeding in the vicinity arrive regularly to steal the show, flying back and forth, right in front of or even behind the almost artificial-looking water curtain. Lively to watch offering good photographic opportunities. With some artistic flying by the birds and the patience of an angel from your side, you can shoot great pictures here.

For birdwatchers, Iceland is paradise on earth. The sheer number of species makes every nature lover fidget in his chair. Just over 350 species have been observed on and around the island. The puffin is undoubtedly the one with the highest cuddly content. More than half the world's population of this feathered clown can be found in Iceland from late May to mid-August.

The vast majority of the birds enjoy a great time along the coastline, while a few loners prefer their privacy retreat to the inhospitable interior. The incredibly beautiful plumed golden plover is one of them. Not always easy to find, but his melancholic whistling soon enables you to catch up with him.

INTO NATURE

It's possible to travel to Iceland with your **own transport**. The Smyril Line ferry company will take you and your four-wheeler from Hirtshals (Northern Denmark) via Tórshavn (Faroe Islands) to Seyðisfjörður (Eastern Iceland). A nice experience, but bear in mind that you'll be on the sea – there and back – for about a week.
https://nl.smyrilline.fo

From October to March you have the best chance of seeing the **northern lights**, an unforgettable natural spectacle.
https://en.vedur.is/weather/forecasts/aurora

Nothing beats wild camping. If you still want a roof over your head, low budget **overnighting** is possible from about 25 euros per person. If you prefer a bit more comfort, the (more expensive) options for accommodation range from guesthouses to hotels or holiday homes.
https://www.booking.com/accommodation/country/is

The Icelandic **winter** is beautiful. Surrounded by the sea, this island has a relatively mild climate. Sudden heavy snowfalls can, however, make travelling heavy-going. Inland roads are then inaccessible, and parts of the ring road may be closed. Also the days are short. You'll have to make do with about 4 hours of light a day, but that light is often sublime.

The spectacular nature of Iceland is something to cherish. That's why more and more travel agencies are doing everything they can to make **sustainable travel** possible in and to this destination. Iceland specialist Askja will map out an adventurous travel plan together with you.
www.askja.nl

Originating out of the belly of our planet, a landscape that breathes the atmosphere of the beginning of time. In Iceland, nature shows its true face all year round. With water and fire as the common thread, you are drawn into a world of primeval landscapes and unadulterated nature. Artists have been at work here. Geysers in the middle of volcanic settings, plains of fluorescent moss and steaming lava fields. Just drive round the ring road and all this beauty rolls out in front of you like a feature film. You get the magic of the light just like that. It's impossible to describe the enormous diversity of this country in a nutshell. Iceland is about making choices and it's not inconceivable that you'll immediately want to plan a second trip. And then you know: the inevitable Iceland virus has struck mercilessly.

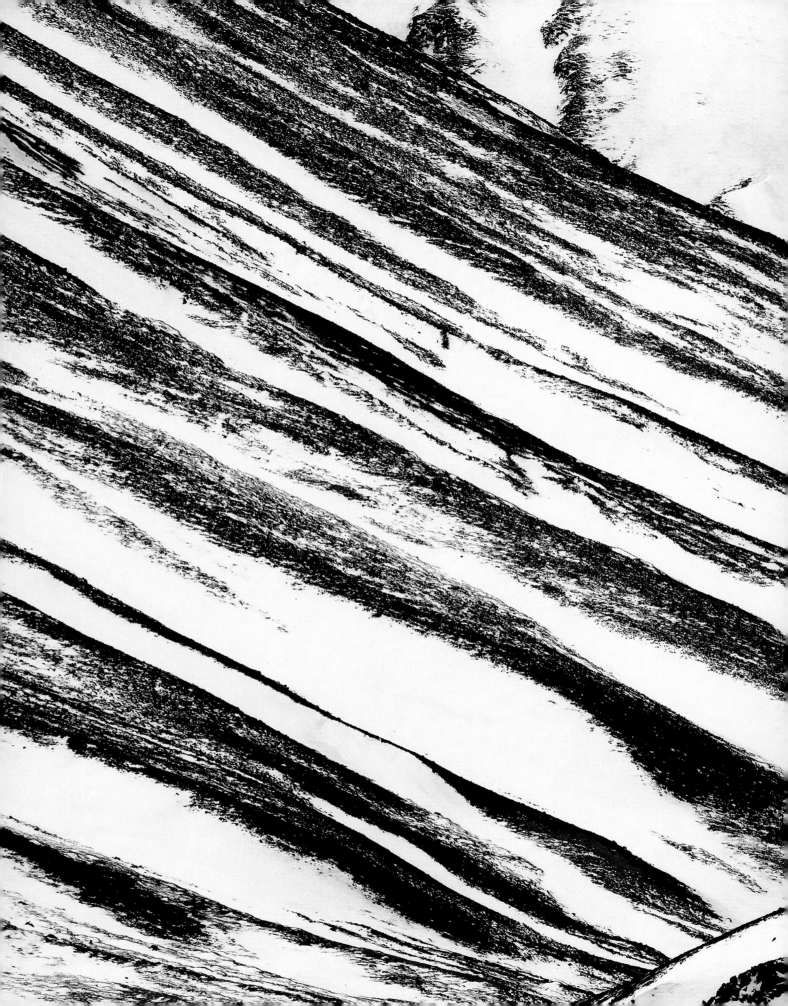

HOTSPOTS

Jökulsárlón
64°04'06.7"N 16°12'38.4"W

South of Vatnajökull National Park, the largest glacier in Europe, lies a glacial lagoon with slowly passing icebergs in the most impossible shapes and shades of blue. It's Southern Iceland's most popular attraction. You'll pass this delightful location on the ring road.

Dyrhólaey
63°23'59.9"N 19°07'33.4"W

An evocative setting which includes the world-famous bird rock where you can see puffins from mid-June to mid-August.

Svartifoss
64°01'38.4"N 16°58'31.0"W

A marvellous waterfall along a spectacular wall of basalt columns. You reach it via the Svartifoss Trail. The nearby Skaftafelljökull Trail takes you close to the Skaftafell glacier. From the Sjónarnýpa viewpoint you have a phenomenal view over the Skaftafellsjökull glacier tongue, over Hvannadalshnjúkur, the highest point in Iceland and the Skeiðarársandur sandy plain.

Hrafntinnusker
63°56'00.0"N 19°10'46.4"W

The Hraftninnusker ice cave consists of centuries-old glacial ice from the Oraefajokull. The cave walls appear transparent and blue. You can reach the cave via the Laugavegurinn Hiking Trail.

Reynisdrangar
63°24'07.5"N 19°02'05.9"W

The mythical black beach at Vík, with the Reynisdrangar rock formations nearby, is a picturesque environment. A journey in itself, a wonderful place to refresh soul and body!

INDRE & CREUSE

FRANCE

LAND OF SNAKE'S HEAD FLOWERS AND PURPLE HERONS

It's late at night when I drive into Rosnay, a small village in the heart of the La Brenne regional park. In my traditional sleeping place, doubled up with hunger, I devour my last hunk of baguette, to the accompaniment of an ear-splitting gaggling. Great, the tree frogs are back en masse this year! And the pair of barn owls is also there, flying silently back and forth with mice for their hungry offspring. A little further on, a skittish pine marten flashes across the road. This feels like coming home. I end the day in style and fall asleep under a starry sky.

The night is short, to say the least: dreamland has only just begun when the first nightingales start their concert. No need to install a new ringtone for my morning wake-up call. Meanwhile, the first wisps of mist loom above the valley where I want to photograph later. With the light intensifying, it's high time to shoot out of my proverbial slippers. Not much later the first pictures are done.

I've been coming to the Indre valley for years now, gradually getting to know the region better than my own back garden. The deeply incised valleys with the meandering rivers Anglin and Creuse in the south contrast starkly with the low-lying marshland in the north. In spring, the watercourses are covered with carpets of white water crowfoot. A mass of gracefully dancing meadow damselflies completes the picture. Someday I'll come here just to relax. Something that unfortunately I've never managed to do: this part of the world has too much to offer. A bevy of amphibians and wacky reptiles, colourful butterflies, crazy mammals and rare plants – it'd be a sin to sit here on my lazy backside!

FEATURED

Perhaps France's best-kept secret, the La Brenne regional park has existed since 1989, featuring a wide variety of forests, marshes and a network of copses and hedgerows. This area is at its best early in the year, as spring slowly awakens, the morning mist still hangs in the valleys and a thousand ponds shine like mirrors in the sun. One glance at an aerial photo or a topographical map speaks volumes and shows just how large the ponds' surface is.

These ponds were created in the Middle Ages for fish farming. From the French Revolution onwards, the profession died out. The ponds dried up, the dams and locks fell into disrepair. Fish farming was restored only from the 1950s onwards. Today there are at least 1200 ponds, from which nature also benefits. Many offer coveted habitats for aquatic plants, birds, reptiles, amphibians and invertebrates. Large parts of the area are now protected.

Today's program is to photograph the black-necked grebe, a trusted inhabitant of La Brenne's many ponds. The loud screeching of a colony of black-headed gulls has kept me awake all night. I don't recommend camping next to a swamp where these troublemakers hold sway. Not yet fully awake, I wriggle into my wetsuit and make my way through the thick reeds in search of my floating hide. Comforted by the thought 'better one leak in my wetsuit than no wetsuit', I finally slide into the water. After some bobbing back and forth, I spot a courting couple in the distance. The sun has meanwhile moved just above the horizon, casting a soft glancing light over the swamp. Centimetre by centimetre I edge towards them, until I'm just a few metres away.

INTO NATURE

At the La Maison du Parc **visitor centre** you'll find all kinds of information about the region. This is *the* starting point for excursions. There are also exhibitions, and the cafeteria terrace offers a fantastic view of the surrounding area. Close to the centre is Le Bouchet castle, at the highest point of La Brenne.
www.parc-naturel-brenne.fr/visitez/la-maison-du-parc

Don't forget your bike. The La Brenne nature park is a **cycling paradise**. It's relatively flat and from your steel horse you see and hear much more. It's the perfect way to explore the region.
www.parc-naturel-brenne.fr

Wild camping is not allowed in France. But the friendly **campsites** make up for this. The municipal campsites are certainly pleasant and very affordable.
www.camping-municipal.org

Spring is the **best period** for a visit to this region. In April, all the birds arrive in dribs and drabs from the south and the amphibians slowly wake up. From May, nature erupts in all its violence. Grasslands are in full bloom, butterflies flutter around en masse, reptiles are running all over the place and the heron colonies are buzzing. The past few years have seen increasing numbers of cranes wintering in the region.

To stay in a wonderful place, in an ecologically and sustainably renovated farm, with super friendly people. You will find this charming base in the heart of the La Brenne regional park.
www.brenneberry.com

In La Brenne, where charming old villages and the peaceful agricultural life are the rule, north and south meet. The area is located in that part of France where continental, Atlantic and southern climate influences can all be felt. This mishmash of weather influences combined with a colourful mosaic of environments results in exceptional biodiversity. Just about every species from the Low Countries can be found here, alongside typical representatives of the Mediterranean environment. Evocative names like green whip snake, European pond turtle, short-toed eagle, stag beetle, meadow saxifrage, green lizard or southern white admiral butterfly roll smoothly over the tongue to make any nature lover swoon.

HOTSPOTS

Réserve Naturelle Nationale de Chérine
46°47'33.9"N 1°11'59.7"E

A nature reserve with the La Maison de la Nature visitor centre on its edge and with several observation points overlooking one of the largest heron colonies of the La Brenne regional park.

Numerous observation cabins offer views of some top locations of the La Brenne regional park: you'll find them at the **Étang Foucault** (46°43'39.4"N 1°13'58.2"E), **Étang de Bellebouche** (46°46'58.7"N 1°18'30.6"E), **Étang Ricot** (46°47'17.2"N 1°11'55.2"E), **Étang Massé** (46°44'27.6"N 1°13'05.1"E) and **Étang de la Sous** (46°47'48.9"N 1°10'32.0"E). For a complete overview you can visit La Maison de la Nature.

Angles-sur-l'Anglin
46°41'37.5"N 0°52'55.4"E

The valley of the Creuse south of the Indre is an exceptional hiking area with an interesting mix of towns, villages and varied landscapes. The picturesque village of Angles-sur-l'Anglin, with its pleasant village square, is considered one of France's most beautiful villages. Close to Rives, the banks of the Anglin are full of orchids.

Azay-le-Ferron and surrounding area
46°50'32.6"N 1°05'43.8"E

This area is known as the place to spot stone curlews, Montagu's harrier and little bustard, although these firecrackers have become really rare. Patiently scour the fields around la Haute Couture.

Les Communeaux
46°40'41.0"N 1°13'42.8"E

A well-hidden nature reserve not far from Rosnay, known for its gigantic quantities of tongue orchids. Thousands of them bloom here in May.

Marais de l'Ozance
46°51'03.0"N 1°16'22.0"E

An alkaline swamp with spectacular biliary vegetation, the last stronghold of the bittern in La Brenne and the site of the rare endemic Brenne orchid.

Vallei van de Indre
46°56'20.0"N 1°18'21.4"E

At the start of spring, in early April, carpets of Snake's head fritillaries turn this valley purple.

JULIJSKE ALPE
SLOVENIA

NATURE ON A LONELY HEIGHT

Shaped by wind and weather, inhospitable and surprisingly colourful in autumn, this mountain range stretching across Italy and Slovenia defies all imagination. It's early November. Packed warm, I trudge in my snowshoes through a thick layer of snow in the Julian Alps. For a moment I imagine myself in higher spheres, overwhelmed by the picturesque landscape as I pace along the shore of a mountain lake. An icy wind howls through the valley and despite the cold I'm sweating. Keep going, I tell myself. I'm approaching the top; the view should be breathtaking. With the spectacular panoramas already flashing through my mind and my head literally and figuratively half in the clouds, I see a group of ibex in the distance. Like true Olympians, they're balanced on a precariously narrow ledge on their way to lower regions. Real daredevils!

I've worn out just about a whole store of boots in many mountainous areas, but this mountain range is just about my favourite. The sharp peaks, the deeply incised gorges and the beautiful forests… In one way or another this place stands out from many others. But it's tough grub here.

In the meantime I've reached the top and am treated to brilliant views. This will be my sleeping place for the night! *A room with a view*, any 5-star hotel room must humbly defer to it. As I doze off, an unadulterated late-night show unfolds in the night sky. Counting sheep is impossible. I think I'm ready for dreamland.

FEATURED

The world's most beautiful mountain range? No doubt everyone has their own opinion in this matter. In any case, the Julian Alps will be near the top of many people's shortlists. Perhaps the most famous mountain range in these Alps, the Dolomites, synonymous with craggy peaks, flowery alpine meadows and delightful nature, is located in Italy. The mountain range has been on the UNESCO World Heritage List since 2009. And deservedly so since the Dolomites offer a surprising mix of Alpine and Mediterranean life. Alpine traditions go hand in hand with Italian lifestyle and cultural diversity, and all that while surrounded by a landscape that simply blows you away. Pack and go!

In addition to phenomenal views, you'll also find quite a few wild animals in the Julian Alps: ptarmigan, golden eagles, marmots and a dizzying number of butterflies and insects, flying, running or jumping all round.

In the mountain acrobat category, the ibex and chamois top the list. You'll find them easily at the higher altitudes, intriguing animals inextricably linked to the high mountains. With the airs of stars, they spring from rock to rock next to the sheer abyss, as if unaware of any danger. In much of their native area, the two species live side by side. The rutting season starts at the beginning of winter with spectacular fights and chases between males. Over the seasons, these animals follow the snow line: in the summer they move about higher in the mountains, in the spring the males can be found in the lower mountain meadows. Who seeks, finds.

INTO NATURE

In Slovenia's Triglav National Park you can overnight in one of the many **mountain huts**. A list of the huts, how to reach them and when they're open can be found at:

https://en.pzs.si/koce.php

With smart **route planning and navigation** technology, the Komoot application maps out the better routes for you, that you can then filter by distance, difficulty and accessibility. Individual routes or full maps can be easily downloaded for offline use.

www.komoot.com

If you plan to go really high up, it's possible you may suffer from **altitude sickness**. Very annoying if you're in the middle of a desolate area. Prepare yourself so that you can prevent it, recognize it and know what to do if it does affect you.

The **weather** in the mountains is changeable and unpredictable. It's wise to stay informed of what's coming so as to anticipate unpleasant surprises.

www.mountain-forecast.com

A compass and solid map material are a good aid in desolate areas. In the mountains too they can come in handy if you are getting lost. Practice your **navigation skills** in advance.

www.wandelpunt.be/navigeren/cursus-kaart-en-kompas

Anders Reizen organizes **sustainable hiking trips** with passion and commitment and with respect for our planet and its inhabitants.

www.andersreizen.be

When the first snow spirals down at the end of autumn, you'll find the most crazy landscape combinations in the mountains. Before they disappear completely, the autumn colours are highlighted one last time by the reflective first layer of snow. For landscape photographers, these are heydays of overtime working. The colours in the wooded valleys are stunning, the valleys have a mysterious atmosphere. An inspiring period!

HOTSPOTS

Triglav National Park
46°22'29.1"N 13°49'42.1"E

The Triglav National Park is a protected area consisting of fantastic mountain peaks, green valleys and several lakes. The park is named after Triglav, the country's highest mountain.

Soča valley
46°20'24.3"N 13°40'53.0"E

The river Soča winds its way through the mighty Soča valley. A scenic breath of fresh air. Enjoy hiking, cycling and kayaking here.

Kranjska Gora
46°28'24.9"N 13°47'02.4"E

The mountain village of Kranjska Gora offers an ideal base for exploring the Triglav National Park. On the shores of nearby Lake Jasna, you'll be blown away by a majestic landscape. A location well-known to photographers.

Zelenci Nature Reserve
46°29'33.2"N 13°44'16.2"E

A stone's throw from Kranjska Gora lies the small but beautiful Zelenci nature reserve. A handsome sample of nature with a beautiful observation point.

Bled
46°21'47.0"N 14°05'31.3"E

One of the most popular destinations in Slovenia is Lake Bled. The best view is from the castle high on the rocks along the lake. In summer it can be very busy, in autumn it's more quiet and the colourful landscape is an extra asset.

INNLANDET
NORWAY

THE MACHOS OF THE FJELLS

The name says it all: Innlandet, the Norwegian interior. In one of Europe's most attractive regions, after a whole day's intensive photography, I'm now searching for somewhere to set up my tent. The fierce gusts and the stony ground don't augur well. Nor does the beautifully coloured reindeer moss, seemingly composed of thousands of packed reindeer antlers, look particularly inviting. Yet it will be my soft bed for the coming night. Putting my head outside in the morning, the feeling of space is total, the view phenomenal. For miles around, brightly coloured birches and glowing moss carpets stretch out in front of me. The superb light with the passing cloud formations gives everything an extra punch. Rich food for landscape photographers indeed.

In the belly of Norway, any number of top areas exist for the choosing, with a large network of adventurous trails connecting one cosy log cabin to the next. You pitch your tent wherever you want, not a troll cares. A piece of Arctic in the south. If you know that a little further on a handful of musk oxen wander around, then no further description is needed. In a few days' time I've an appointment with this powerhouse, the macho of the fjells, a meeting I'm really looking forward to!

The addiction level of this part of Norway is quite high. Here you can wander for days without meeting a single lost soul. In a rugged landscape, occasional unhinged reindeer and a lone moose keep your focus sharp. Deep in the tundra the crackling call of a ptarmigan. In the icy water, a white-throated dipper dives after the scarce insects as if its life depended on it. If you thought you were coming for a lazy holiday, you're wrong. There's so much to experience and discover in this part of the north, it's enough to drive you nuts!

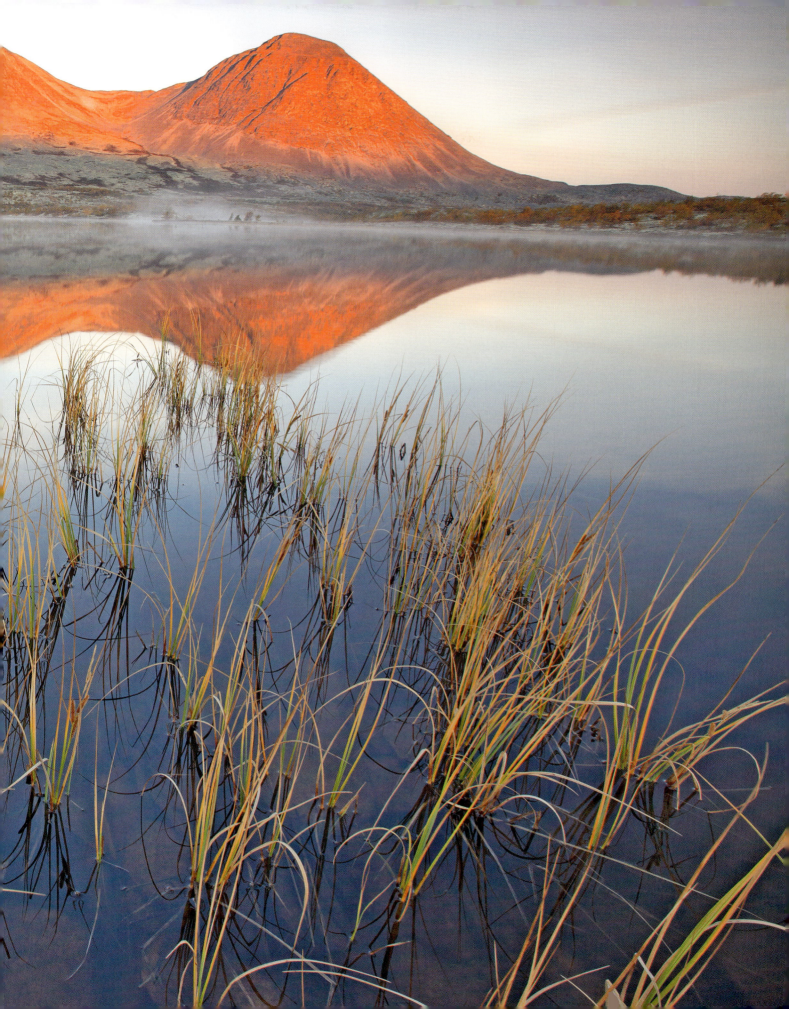

INTO NATURE

A very nice portal with lots of **practical information** about the region is provided by the Nasjonalparkriket, the national parks authority.

www.nasjonalparkriket.no

Want to know everything about the best **huts** in Norway? Then knock on the door of The Norwegian Trekking Association.

https://english.dnt.no/routes-and-cabins

Just for seeing the **musk oxen**, many people place Dovrefjell National Park right at the top of their wish list. The park's website offers a wealth of useful information.

https://dovrefjell-sunndalsfjella.no

If you don't want to fly or travel with your own car, you can take the **train** from various departure points to Otta, Dombas, Hjerkinn or Kongsvold. Buses run from the station in Otta to the edge of the national parks.

https://entur.no

Glide silently past the majestic landscape and watch everything in slow motion. In recent years, kayaking has become a popular outdoor activity in Norway. Several rivers in the region are suitable for **kayaking** in a unique setting.

www.visitnorway.com/things-to-do/outdoor-activities/canoeing-kayaking

Want to discover more places in this region under the guidance of a team of enthusiastic and **experienced travel specialists**? Nordic's travel designers take the necessary time to meet your wishes.

www.nordic.be

Clouds sail swiftly across the Norwegian tundra. I'm exploring Dovrefjell in search of the legendary musk ox. Brute force on four legs is the best way I can describe these freaks. Here lives the only population in Europe, introduced here in the first half of the last century. Although it closely resembles a bovine, the musk ox is actually more closely related to the goat and sheep.

In Dovrefjell, even fanatical top athletes will come out in a sweat. From the valley it's straight up, arriving a little later into a grand landscape. After hours of staring, there's not a single ox in sight. It's like searching for a needle in a haystack. However, the incessant wind and fatigue are quickly forgotten when a little later I catch a first glimpse of a group in the distance. Cautiously I try to approach them, until one of the furry four-legged creatures warns me that this sub-arctic piece of nature does indeed belong to them. A nearby wheatear also notices it and skedaddles off on stocking feet. I also wisely step back. I'd rather not get into trouble with this long-haired work-shy beast.

FEATURED

Tundra, a bitter wind and a quick succession of heavy showers: many people will thank you kindly for this. Yet these are the basic ingredients of the astonishing sample of nature that will form my operations base for the next few days. I'm on my way to Rondane, Norway's oldest national park. During the car ride I feed my eyes richly. The scenery is something to die for!

With several peaks above 2000 meters, Rondane is known as an adventurous hiking paradise. This time I'm being really ambitious. From the parking lot I start my journey through a sparkling landscape of bubble moss and colourful dwarf birches, after which I work up a serious sweat, climbing straight up to Rondeslottet, the highest mountain in this park. The view at the top is nothing short of phenomenal! With the clear weather I have luck on my side and I can even see right as far as the Jotunheimen and Forrollhogna national parks on the horizon.

HOTSPOTS

Rondane National Park
61°55'52.8"N 9°47'18.5"E

One entrance to the national park is to the southwest of Rondane, near the small hamlet of Mysusaeter. Various walks and cycling routes across the plateau depart from the car park.

Dovrefjell National Park
62°21'50.3"N 9°06'20.6"E

Dovrefjell, together with Sunndalsøra, forms a large national park in the centre of Norway. A beautiful hiking area with the famous Snøhettapeak, an undulating mountain landscape with winding rivers and – with some detective work – musk oxen or an Arctic fox.

Sohlbergplassen
61°52'49.2"N 10°11'07.8"E

A viewing platform overlooking Lake Atnasjøen, with the mountains of the Rondane National Park as background. The place is named after artist Harald Sohlberg, painter of the famous *Winter Night in Rondane*.

Snøhetta observation point
62°13'26.3"N 9°29'24.2"E

Catch a glimpse of Snøhetta, rising 2.286 metres above sea level. From the parking lot, after a short climb you reach this sample of world-class architecture, a crown jewel that is part of the Norwegian Wild Reindeer Centre. In 2011, the building was proclaimed 'World Building of the Year'.

Jotunheimen National Park
61°33'16.8"N 8°29'27.0"E

Explore the land of the giants in Jotunheimen National Park. Here you'll find not only Norway's two highest mountains, but also some of Scandinavia's nicest hiking trails. You can also explore the park by car. In this case, you'll drive on the Sognefjellet, the highest mountain road in Scandinavia, with fantastic views along the way.

THE ICEMAN AND THE SHUFFLING WIND

It must be somewhere in early January when, with some reluctance, I roll out of my warm sleeping bag after an icy night in my van. At minus 12 °C the thermometer is seriously in the red by Belgian standards. No one's eager to brave this freezing cold at dawn and dusk with a heavy backpack full of glassware. But there's no wind and with a fresh pack of snow having fallen last night, the photographic conditions look so promising that I can't pass up the opportunity. Shortly after, the fresh snow crunches beneath my feet. A wildlife photographer's life can be a hard one.

The High Fens are impressive. In this barren corner of Belgium, I bow my head reverently as I cross this endless peat landscape on the narrow, weathered decking paths. As far as the eye can see, nothing but forest, peat and swamp. Given the severe climate, even mountain species survive here. As I make my way through the snow and a shuffling, icy wind blows right in my face, I can imagine it.

I'm wary of the virgin snow carpet and decide to strictly follow the marked trails. The peat bogs are not harmless terrain. Before you know it, you've lost your bearings and you're continuing your earthly existence as 'the Iceman'. No thanks, photographing winter landscapes seems a worthy alternative to me. And with these short days I'd better not waste time, because before you know it the day will be over. Indeed, it's already dark when I arrive back at my snow-covered vehicle a few hours later. After a quick bite, the choice for the down of my sleeping bag is quickly made. A fresh layer of snow meanwhile readies everything for a new start the next morning.

FEATURED

The High Fens in winter dress are a real tourist draw. Immediately after the first snow has fallen, hundreds of sports enthusiasts eagerly strap on their skis and a horde of nature photographers descend in search of the ultimate landscape image. Noir Flohay may have been photographed over and over, yet this piece of landscape art continues to inspire many photographers to create sublime imagery, with which to steal a medal at one of the many prestigious photo competitions.

These dead trees are the remains of a pine forest that was planted in 1852 but burned down in 2011. The trees are also called 'crolés sapés' or curly spruce. This abstract place comes into its own on a cold, misty winter's day.

Here, on the roof of Belgium, biodiversity has long been written large. An astonishing arsenal of animals and plants await you here, with mother nature offering a rich selection of rarities: rare peat mosses, pearl-bordered fritillary butterflies, bog rosemary, black grouse, nutcracker, gentian, and you may even bump into the extremely rare lynx. All rarities you'll be hard put to see elsewhere in Belgium.

The High Fens are also the right place for the exceptionally rare Tengmalm's owl. This bird lives in the same spruce forests as the spotted nutcracker, where it hunts at dusk for small rodents and large insects. The best chance to spot this owl is in the spring, from March to May. Searching out this skittish bird of prey usually takes some time, but with tips from fellow birdwatchers and some good detective work you stand a good chance of success.

INTO NATURE

The 'Centre Nature Botrange' **visitor centre** is your base for exploring the High Fens nature park. Brochures and maps are available from the tourist office.
www.centrenaturebotrange.be

The High Fens form a beautiful **walking area**. Numerous marked routes lead you into it. You explore the area along footpaths and a network of timber duckboards. Instructive information boards point you in the right direction.
https://botrange.be

Of course a **winter** visit is more than worth the effort, and you can also go into the area with skis if there is enough snow.
www.ostbelgien.eu/en/what-to-do/wintersport/ski-centres

The High Fens are a very popular **cycling area**. No less than 850 km of cycling routes with various cycling nodes have been mapped out. A very pleasant alternative for exploring the area is the rail bike. This attraction is also suitable for wheelchair users and families with children.
www.railbike.be

If you can't see the woods for the trees, vzw Wallonia has published a wealth of **practical information** about the region.
https://walloniabelgiumtourism.co.uk

HOTSPOTS

Fagne de Polleur
50°30'30.3"N 6°04'15.8"E

This piece of nature houses the remains of an old peat distillery and has been protected since 1984. A must is the route over the boardwalk starting from the Mont Rigi inn.

Vallée de la Hoëgne
50°30'28.6"N 5°57'37.4"E

The Hoëgne is a tributary of the Vesdre on the edge of the High Fens. The valley offers superb walks. In autumn in particular, this is a real walker's paradise.

Brackvenn
50°33'55.4"N 6°10'15.8"E

Fagne de Brackvenn, one of the most beautiful areas of the High Fens, lies on the Belgian-German border. A long wooden boardwalk takes you through peat bogs and marshland. This is one of Belgium's last raised bogland sites.

Signal de Botrange
50°30'12.4"N 6°05'39.7"E

Around the Signal de Botrange lives the last Belgian population of the black grouse, one of the iconic inhabitants of the High Fens. The chances of getting to see them are slim; but from the observation point you can already scan the area. Botrange is also the starting point for numerous walks.

Hertogenwald and valley of the Soor
50°34'55.7"N 6°03'23.0"E

The Hertogenwald lies on the German-Belgian border. It's a gigantic forest, in which it's easy to get lost. The Hertogenwald walk takes you along babbling brooks and surprising panoramas.

Let's be honest: few biotopes are as intriguing as a forest. The unfamiliar sounds, exciting forest stories and mythical mushrooms turn every forest walk into a memorable experience. And when you also bump into a wild boar, the adventure is complete. These animals are still well represented in the Eastern Cantons. You know they're there, but it's still a shock every time a gang of these grunting, squabbling cronies cross your path. You'd better keep out of the way. Still, I like them, those bastards, with their funny pyjamas.

Wild boars have poor vision, but they smell all the better. They're real detectives. With their hypersensitive snout they

know exactly where slugs, worms and other soil-dwellers are hiding. The cute piglets are born between February and June. It's better to steer well clear of their mothers during this period. A private conversation with one is as unwelcome as a toothache.

IN THE FOOTSTEPS OF BRUNO THE BEAR

It's midnight and I'm in the middle of a sea of peat fluff, folded double in a hide that is far too small. Only with a shoehorn will I be able to free myself from this cramped situation. A few steps away a couple of young brown bears are tussling with each other. I hold my breath and squeeze my arm just to be sure. For a moment I even imagine myself as David Attenborough shooting his umpteenth spectacular nature documentary. In the background the trumpet call of a lone crane. Its slowly expanding echo dies in the peat. Afterwards that deafening, ear-hurting silence once again.

With this intense bear adventure still resonating in my mind, I continue my way north. Travelling around Finland means countless moments of wonder and at least as many unforgettable impressions. From behind the wheel I see the immense backdrop of the Finnish taiga with its jetblack fens, crystal clear lakes and swampy birch forests pass by. Besides my target, Bruno the bear, I hope to catch the rare red-flanked bluetail and the wolverine during this trip. So far without success. Still, I'm happy as a kid with a handful of bony elk, a mysterious great grey owl, and several groups of bustling grouse. Wondering what else my path will cross.

In this part of Northern Europe I'm totally immersed in the rhythm of nature. Stress only overwhelms me when I meet some rare animal, I sleep when the sun is at its zenith. My sense of time disappears like snow in the sun, my biological clock takes over. The north takes hold of me again.

Never-ending white plains in winter, like colorful paintings in autumn, graced by cheerfully yodelling wood sandpipers in spring, peatlands may seem flat and dull at first glance, but they are anything but. The silence is unreal, the views unparalleled. The curtains of mosquitoes and the fumes of rotting eggs are secondary. Walking across the peat is magical, like stepping over a waterbed. Fun, but not without danger, because there are admittedly better disappearing tricks. So don't stray too far from the trails. In this way too, this extremely fragile vegetation remains unharmed. Knowing that the packets of metres-thick peat have taken thousands of years to grow, a modicum of respect is in order. The peat mosses may be tiny, but together they form grand landscapes, vital for nature and the climate.

The soundtrack of the far north, that must be the cry of the red-throated diver. Just for the cry I would have travelled this long distance. Nor is this bird a wimp. Every year this glittering appearance exchanges its wintering area for a pool of ice-cold water in order to raise its brood in peace. This particular diver knows how to choose its habitat. No luxury required. Their nest? A meagre heap of plant material into which Mrs Diver can lay a handful of eggs. For me this is one of the most beautiful birds on earth. Perfection doesn't exist, but the plumage of the red-throated diver comes pretty close. Finished with an eye for detail and polished with utmost precision.

INTO NATURE

A wealth of **information** about the national parks, nature reserves and visitor centres in Northern Finland can be found at www.nationalparks.fi.

The roadside café Neljan Tuulen Tupa north of Kaamanen is known by birdwatchers and photographers for its **feeders** that attract lots of birds, including the pine grosbeak and other beauties.
www.neljantuulentupa.com

If you want to prepare or stay informed of what is to be seen and where, it would be a good idea to check the past few days' **observations**.
https://finland.observation.org

Siida (the Cultural and Nature Centre of the Sámi) and **Sajos** (the Center of Sámi Culture and Administration) are both located in Inari. There you can learn more about the Sami culture and the natural wonders of the far north.
https://siida.fi

The **winters** in Northern Finland are legendary but very cold, especially along the Russian border. Be ready for temperatures down to -50 °C.

Together with local partners in Finnish Lapland, five passionate travel enthusiasts work all year round on travel concepts with a focus on **nature experience** to offer everyone a unique travel experience.
https://laplandtravel.com

FEATURED

They're shy, lead a withdrawn life and usually live in the most inaccessible places. Meetings don't happen just like that. That is exactly what makes brown bears so unmatched and extraordinary. A mysterious atmosphere and icy silence set the scene for a mythical moment. Out of the corner of my eye I see mother bear with two chubby cubs strolling from the forest edge into the peat. They're clearly wary, preferring to avoid the oversized male crouching against a tree in the distance. However, the colossus turns out to only have eyes for himself, the back massage is visibly doing him good, the tree moans. The youngsters don't mind it too much and play all kinds of crazy tricks close to my hide. I'm splitting my sides with laughter.

HOTSPOTS

Kilpisjärvi
69°00'48.5"N 20°49'57.5"E

In Kilpisjärvi you're in the middle of the tundra. An excellent area for winter trekking, with a network of hiking huts.

Kevo Nature Reserve
69°41'2.6"N 27°4'40.7"E

The 62 km multi-day hike through the Kevo nature reserve runs largely through the Kevo Gorge. Highly recommended if you're in the area.

Pyha-Luosto National Park
67°045'1.0"N 26°55'28.3"E

This park encompasses Finland's southernmost fjell range. The Luontopolku nature trail is very varied. You cross old forests with large variations in elevation, fields with boulders and a peat bog with a watchtower (Tunturiaapa). Be sure to visit the Naava visitor centre as well.

Valtavaara
66°11'14.5"N 29°11'32.3"E

Valtavaara is a very good place for spotting the rare red-flanked bluetail. From this mountain you can also enjoy vast views across the region.

Urho Kekkonen National Park
68°09'59.3"N 28°15'00.5"E

A gigantic 255.000 hectare park stretching all the way to the Russian border. The area has three visitor centres. Four walks start from the Koilliskaira visitor centre, of which the one from Kuukkeli to the Little Tankavaara mountain is recommended.

Oulanka National Park
66°22'28.5"N 29°19'28.5"E

Discover the power of water in the rugged landscape of Oulanka National Park along the Karhunkierros Trail. The suspension bridges lead you to some impressive waterfalls.

Kiilopää Fell
68°20'29.0"N 27°30'09.8"E

One of the few fjells where you can see and photograph the rare Eurasian dotterel. Climb to the top of the mountain while scanning the flanks all the time. With a bit of luck you'll spot this beautiful bird.

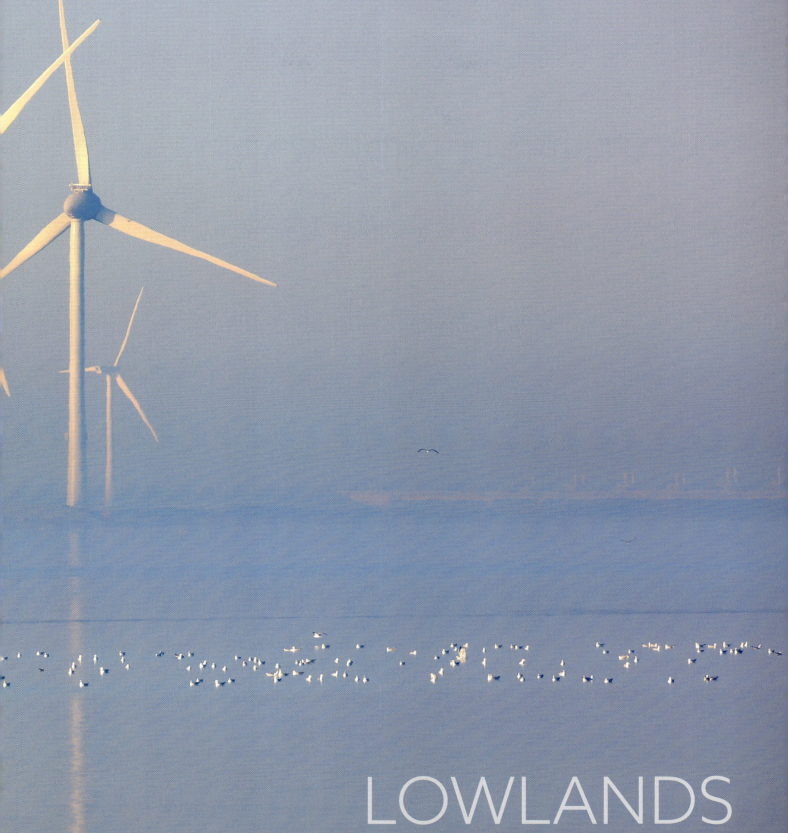

LOWLANDS
THE NETHERLANDS

THE BOKKEGAT
AND THE PLOMPE TOREN

Look! A group of long-tailed ducks! I've found them with my telescope, bobbing leisurely on the high seas, still in their splendid dress. At Brouwersdam, birdwatching is quite an easy task, especially in winter. A trained birdwatcher quickly ticks off dozens of species from his wish list. For any self-respecting birdwatcher, this place is a must-visit.

Flauwers en Wevers, Bokkegat, the Zwaakse Weel, the Quackjeswater, Neeltje Jans or the Zak van Zuid-Beveland: these top areas not only sound fantastic, they're also part of the extensive nature network that has been developed in recent years in this corner of the Netherlands with its witty names. With the ambitious 'Tureluur Plan', people in Zeeland have seriously rolled up their sleeves to give back to nature what it is entitled to: space. The result is stunning. Seals, tree frogs, clouds of waders, rare plants, thousands of howling migrating geese, porpoises, yes even flamingos are now at home here. Definitely the better line-up of the Netherlands annual Lowlands festival. What a top billing!

I've just retraced my steps to visit the Plompe Toren, another nice name. From the tower I gaze down at the Koudekerkse Inlaag nature reserve, which also seems to be bubbling with life. The view is phenomenal. In the distance, the large sandbanks in the Oosterschelde poke their noses above water, further away giant windmills dominate the skyline. A huge tanker drifts slowly past, while the kilometre-long lock complex keeps close watch on water levels. Here, people and nature seem to go hand in hand. A great collaboration!

FEATURED

Unloved, unknown, and yet. In nature, so many little creatures crawl and fly around – you know they're there but pay little or no attention to them. They come in all shapes and colours: hairy, armoured, camouflaged, striped or plain, you name it... A cheerful mishmash that you can only admire.

You can also come across the natterjack toad in amongst the rich variety of nature in Zeeland. Its reclusive way of life has everything to do with this. You mightn't expect it right away, but this pioneer species is now a regular customer in Zeeland's dunes and sandy areas from spring onwards. Getting to actually see the animals is another story. If you prick up your ears, you may have a better chance. Especially in the evening after a rainy period it's worth listening: the rattling choir of toads can often be heard from more than a kilometre away.

INTO NATURE

In Zeeland you can admire nature undisturbed from various **observation huts**.
www.vogelkijkhut.nl

The **Tij bird observatory** is an impressive observation point. With the support of the Haringvliet Dream Fund, Vogelbescherming Nederland and Natuurmonumenten have 'laid' this giant egg on the edge of the Scheelhoek bird reserve.
www.natuurmonumenten.nl/natuurgebieden/scheelhoek/vogelkijkpunten/vogelobservatorium-tij

Water levels are very determinative for seeing animals. Check the situation in advance if you want to go looking for seals or waders, for example.
www.rijkswaterstaat.nl/en/water

Oosterschelde National Park is the Netherlands' largest national park. The range of activities on offer is simply huge.
www.np-oosterschelde.nl
www.ontdekdeoosterschelde.nl

Seals are everywhere in Zeeland. You often see them taking forty winks on the tidal mud flats of the Oosterschelde at low tide. Want to see the animals close up? A nature guide will take you on a **seal safari** cruise of two hours.
www.frisiarondvaarten.nl

Looking for the best **bird areas**? Several websites can lend a hand here.
www.birdingplaces.eu

The nature festival of the Low Countries. That's Zeeland. Birdwatching is an excellent idea here at any time of the year. So easy that you can even watch birds to your heart's content from your car. But don't forget to stretch your legs every now and then. From the many bird hides and lookout points in this region you will undoubtedly see more.

Those roguish Dutch know damned well how to do things. Here, they've fully restored the natural wealth that has been lost in many other places. Creeks have been uncovered again, the salty seepage water is no longer pumped out and nature management has been expertly optimised. With all the consequences: a bird paradise where many mouths water with admiration. Take those binoculars down from the shelf and feast your eyes!

HOTSPOTS

Koudekerkse Inlaag
51°41′05.0″N 3°46′26.9″E

From the Plompe Toren you have an astounding view of this nature reserve and the surrounding area. In the autumn, this interesting bird area turns red with marsh samphire.

Kwade Hoek
51°50′24.5″N 3°59′48.9″E

In the Kwade Hoek, the varied landscape offers interesting transitions from salt to brackish and fresh water. You'll discover lots of birds and a great diversity of plants, including orchids, along the unpaved footpaths.

Moriaanshoofd
51°41′00.6″N 3°50′37.1″E

The Prunjepolder is one of Zeeland's largest nature reserves and a good example of nature restoration under the Tureluur Plan. Close to the Flauwers en Wevers Inlagen (inter-dike area), you can enjoy a beautiful panorama from the wooden watchtower.

Scheelhoek
51°48′47.1″N 4°03′34.4″E

Birds make a beeline for this major bird sanctuary just behind the Haringvliet locks on the island of Goeree-Overflakkee, with the must-see new Tij observatory.

Quackjeswater
51°50′51.5″N 4°04′39.5″E

This dune lake is known for its nesting spoonbills. In the meantime, more than 200 nests have been counted. Not far from the entrance to the area is a lookout point offering spectacular views of the colony.

Battenoord
51°42′19.9″N 4°07′41.7″E

Every year, near the little harbour of Battenoord, a group of waders that you would not immediately expect winters here: flamingos. This is one of the better vantage points for spotting these exotic birds.

The Verdronken Land van Saeftinghe may be located in the farthest corner of Zeeland, but for many nature lovers it's a permanent fixture in their winter diaries, for many animals a comfortable home. This great tidal area will blow every visitor's mind. In this immeasurable area of mud flats and salt marshes, they have been fighting the water for centuries, with varying degrees of success. Today, nature can take its course and you can see what the landscape must have looked like before humans left their mark. Diked in centuries ago, now recaptured by the sea, this is one of the few remaining dynamic landscapes in the region.

SCYTHE-WIELDING FARMERS AND BENT-CROOKED LADIES

Once past the German-Polish border, the landscape quickly changes. Roads get worse, villages smaller, nature more exuberant. The planned stops promise well: great reed warblers singing in godforsaken reed beds and courting common snipes whirring above my head. Meanwhile, I'm brutally killing a handful of mosquitoes. They probably won't be the last.

The next evening I'm already exploring somewhere along the Belarusian border. Although the road builders have done their utmost, you can safely take the word 'road' with a serious pinch of salt. Bumpy gravel roads lead me through a desolate region of picturesque villages and structured deciduous forests. Fantastic to know that wolves, lynx and many other rare mammals still roam here undisturbed. In our western parts they have long disappeared from the scene.

To a melodious concert of crazy golden orioles, a couple of black storks screw steadily into the air and a family of hazel grouse hurry across the road. An old, bent-crooked lady with a radiant smile watches from her doorway as I go into ecstasy as a lesser spotted eagle flies into the woods. What a strange fellow, she must have thought. She waves kindly and shuffles back inside.

In north-eastern Poland, the clock seems to have turned back a century. Horses and carts, scythe-wielding farmers and haystacks characterize the small-scale landscape. Nature and agriculture still go hand in hand, far from any hustle and bustle. Let's hope this authentic piece of Europe will stay preserved for a long time to come.

In wide bends, the river Biebrza ambles through an unsullied labyrinth of reed beds, colourful meadows and soaking wet swamps. No gently babbling brook, but a mighty river full of aquatic plants that flows 164 kilometres through a marvellous environment, the setting for many an old folk tale and where large mammals hide. Meanwhile, this river valley treats every visitor to a generous portion of high-profile nature.

Established in 1993, the Biebrzański National Park offers the largest intact peat bog ecosystem in Central Europe. In contrast to the swamps in neighbouring European countries, all attempts to drain and cultivate the wet soils of the Biebrza Valley have failed. Thanks to increasing environmental awareness, its future still seems assured. This is one of the most important places for waterfowl and waders in Europe,

with the rare ruff as a highlight and now the area's mascot. Around a tenth of Central Europe's ruff population comes to breed here.

The European bison seems to have walked right out of pre-history. After many years of heavy weather, this iconic four-legged friend is making a real comeback on the European continent. At the beginning of this century, they could still be counted on one hand. Nature conservation organizations then joined forces and set up a reintroduction program. Animals were released into the remaining natural wilderness of central and eastern Europe.

The bison is an engine for the preservation of valuable nature. While grazing, it models the landscape and fulfils to perfection its role as a talented landscape architect. Many animals and plants benefit from the presence of these hairy herbivores. Through its diet, this tough buffalo not only helps maintain an attractive puzzle of forested areas and grasslands, but also creates ecological corridors along which not only itself, but also many other animals can move undisturbed.

INTO NATURE

Winter is the ideal season for **animal trackers**. Especially in the snow, paw prints are easy to find. In the Obsidentify app, you upload a photo, and immediately know what you've found.
https://waarnemingen.be/apps/obsidentify

The period to see **European bison** is April. At that time of year they often move around in large herds, with the view not yet obstructed by dense foliage. The largest population lives in the forest of Białowieża.
https://whc.unesco.org/en/list/33

Travelling by **train** to Poland is affordable and relaxed. Once there, you have to come to terms with a somewhat more difficult-to-navigate public transport system.
www.interrail.eu/nl/plan-your-trip/tips-and-tricks/trains-europe/trains-country/trains-poland

Proper **preparation** is everything here. Consult travel reports in advance. With some searching you can find several online.
www.cloudbirders.com

A good **mosquito repellent** is your best friend in the nature reserves from spring onwards. Preferably bring it from home because the spray is often difficult to obtain locally.

The Wild Poland organisation helps people reconnect with nature and the real, untouched Poland. It brings together various experienced **local nature guides** and avid nature lovers. They all share one thing: a great passion for wildlife.
https://wildpoland.com

FEATURED

Lynx lead secretive lives. They roam the forest, the larger and denser it is the better. If possible without too many snoopers. The lynx remains an inscrutable beast with a gaze that sees through everything and everyone. Of the size of a large cat and with an unsurpassed degree of agility, despite its somewhat clumsy appearance.

Being a lynx is a special craft. Hanging out in the wild, on your own, constantly spying around for a tasty morsel. It's a shrewd hunter, a cunning cat with a phenomenal hunting technique. As hunters, Mr and Mrs Lynx are unrivalled. But as a species they're having a hard time of it. Man has severely reduced their hunting grounds in recent years. And that's precisely what this beautiful cat is so sensitive to. In Eastern Poland there's fortunately still plenty of room for this fascinating predator. Let's keep it that way.

HOTSPOTS

Brzeziny Kapickie
53°31'55.0"N 22°43'13.0"E

An interesting place for spotting mammals. Home port for, among others, beavers, moose and red deer. There's also a wolf pack, although the chances of seeing it are small.

Osowiec Fort II
53°29'30.0"N 22°38'22.0"E

Many people come here to visit the Russian military fortresses from World War I, but this is also a great place for birdwatching. Here you can find the yellow-bellied toad.

Grzędy & Red Bog
53°37'55.0"N 22°46'24.0"E

From here you can take interesting walks through forest, sand dunes and marshland with a chance of meeting moose and black grouse. Wolves and lynx are spotted here almost every year.

Goniądz
53°29'28.0"N 22°44'01.0"E

The largest town in the Biebrza valley. As a centrally located higher point in the area, it's an excellent base for great excursions.

Brzostowo
53°19'01.0"N 22°27'49.0"E

A beautiful place to enjoy the sunrise and sunset. Viewpoints and towers offer a great view of the Biebrza valley. Well-known to ornithologists.

LAS EXTREMADURAS

SPAIN

FRAGRANT SPANISH LAVENDER UNDER CORK TREES

Not too fast! Feed the eyes and enjoy, with the occasional good siesta in between. I've only just arrived in Spain and I already feel like a true Spaniard again. Living with the sun, up early and late to bed, with an extended break in between. These southerners have got it spot on; a daily schedule that fits wonderfully with that of a nature photographer in his search for the optimum light.

As always, I cross Spain to the rhythm of its omnipresent nature. It comes at you naturally from all sides: the mighty Pyrenees have not completely disappeared from view when I enter a parched Aragonese steppe landscape. In the distance, another mountain range looms on the horizon. I'm on my way to the region of Extremadura, where nature reigns supreme and tasty tapas and wines not to be sneezed at are at the top of many menus. But if you thought that I was there to put my feet under a table, then you will be disillusioned. Soon fields full of Spanish lavender and weathered cork oaks will be served up to me, with masses of loose stones under my feet.

It's time for the real work. I go treasure-hunting for otters, great bustards and Spanish festoon butterflies. The menu here consists of the best that nature can offer. Touring, photographing and admiring are my main activities. I've already been able to intercept a few groups of cranes that have lingered here this winter and are now travelling to their breeding grounds. They must be pretty much the last ones. The great bustards, bee-eaters, hoopoes and other exotic-looking birds will soon change the guard. The prospects are far from bad. For a few weeks I'm once again able to indulge my passion for nature, happy to roll up my sleeves for a portion of unforgettable nature experience.

Viva España!

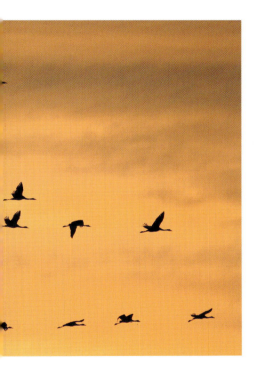

INTO NATURE

Travel reports give you ideas and set you on your way to often less known places. You'll find a lot of information online with which to prepare thoroughly.
 www.birdtours.co.uk

In many places in Spain it's still pitch dark at night. Then it's time for **stargazing**. A moment to brush up on your knowledge. Apps lend you a hand: Sky Map, Nasa App or Night Sky Lite. All apps work with augmented reality: you hold your phone up in the direction of the stars and all available information appears on your screen.

Classic camping spots can be found everywhere. For **small-scale campsites** you can visit Campspace. This is your guide to special mini campsites, often at people's private properties.
https://campspace.com/en/discover/camping-in-spain

Hot, hotter, hottest. In Spain, temperatures often rise high and the **light** quickly becomes too harsh. Head out early in the morning or just before sunset to take photos. The temperatures are also more pleasant then. And not only is the light softer, but it's also very quiet.

The campsites can be in inhospitable regions, but always they offer you a pleasant place to stay. For a **cosy place** in the middle of nature with full comfort, visit www.nature.house. In addition, with your booking you contribute to local nature projects.

Sun, sea and beach. Mention Spain, and these are the first things that come into the average person's mind. Yet this Mediterranean country has more than that in store, with many protected natural areas, all surprisingly different. Nature in Spain exudes both calm and agitation, it's dynamic and ever-changing. In summer a real baking oven, in other seasons a feast of colours and shapes, vibrant with life.

With its Mediterranean climate, Spain is home to very unique fauna and flora. Species that have long since disappeared from other areas put in very regular appearances. Hoopoes, vultures and sandgrouses fly around your ears, even if you actually came to identify the many butterflies. Multi-taskers clearly have the advantage here. The range of nature is so extensive that you usually come with more than one pair of binoculars.

FEATURED

The tropically coloured bee-eater looks like he's been cut out of a charming picture book. In large parts of Spain you still have a considerable chance of spotting this remarkable phenomenon. Without too much effort, because with their attractive outfit and their graceful glide you'll recognize them from thousands. If you see one flying, it is likely that its buddies will follow.

For these colony breeders, the warm southern climate is a blessing. Insects, which still fly around abundantly here, are as birds for a cat and are plucked from the air with playful ease by these cunning flying artists. As an insect it's therefore better not to venture too close, because in a flash you've become the food of the begging chicks who, a little further on, are peeping into their parents' ears in an ordinary pile of sand.

HOTSPOTS

La Serena
38°40'09.2"N 5°38'59.7"W

A steppe area south-east of the towns of Don Benito and Villanueva de la Serena. Numerous side roads are worth exploring and always provide beautiful opportunities for observing various typical steppe species.

Trujillo
39°27'33.4"N 5°52'48.9"W

Trujillo is well worth a visit. If not for the historic buildings, the city walls and the castle, then for sighting the lesser kestrel and the pallid swift.

Barrueco de Abajo
39°25'15.7"N 6°30'02.7"W

Just west of Cáceres in the Malpartida region is the Los Barruecos National Park. Huge artistically-shaped boulders create an almost surreal landscape. The nesting white storks nearby are an attraction in themselves.

Plains east of Santa Marta de Magasca
39°30'49.8"N 6°05'03.0"W

Here you can explore the vast plains of Santa Marta. There are two marked walks in the area. On the walk between the stone walls, you'll be treated to a beautiful view of the region.

Monfragüe National Park
39°49'40.9"N 6°03'00.6"W

Monfragüe, consisting of a steep ridge running alongside the dammed-up Tagus, is one of Europe's best bird of prey areas. The park is said to be home to more than 170 bird species, including several rarities like the Spanish imperial eagle and the cinereous vulture.

HIGHLANDS
SCOTLAND

ROCK 'N ROLL WITH BAGPIPES

In an almost deserted harbour some rough fishermen are admiring their rich catch. A little further on you'll soon be able to taste samples of their daily fresh haul, sitting at the counter on worn barstools in an equally desolate pub. For enthusiasts a large peaty whiskey is also available. Behind the bar a barrel of a man; a set of bagpipes wouldn't look out of place. It's pouring with rain outside, so I take my chance and join the 'table'. For those who still have doubts: I'm on tour in Scotland.

I'm hoping the weather gods will be a bit more clement in the coming days, as I want to get out into the wide world as soon as possible. After all, the high level of rock 'n roll of Scotland only really comes into its own when you stand foursquare with both feet in it: the wind in your hair, the eternal murmur of the sea in your ears, the smell of cut peat in your nostrils, and with screaming seagulls forming the backdrop.

After the delicious fish and the warm introduction at the bar – the whiskey I prudently turned down – I continue my way, despite the persistent rain, down the narrow, winding lanes along the sea. Absolutely magnificent! Except for a herd of fleeing sheep and a drowned-looking red deer, nothing but a dazzling coastal landscape. From the higher flanks, the view of the unique coastline and the vast peatlands is delightful. The sun has come out a few times now and I can even see the Hebrides peeping out on the distant horizon. The cloud formations become more and more dramatic with pitch-black cumulus clouds against the increasingly pink sky. Just the way I want it! The camera is allowed out of its trusted backpack for the first time.

I'm not surprised that, not so long ago, Scotland was declared the most beautiful region on this globe. Here you set foot in one of the largest contiguous wildernesses in Europe. One large amusement park for nature lovers and passionate nature photographers.

FEATURED

With its sharp peaks it rises triumphantly above everything and everyone: Old Man of Storr on the Isle of Skye is a landmark of genius. It's no surprise that this place has been the setting for several blockbusters. According to one of many legends, a giant lived in the Trotternish Ridge. When he died, he is said to have been buried entirely, except for his thumb, which now rises above the landscape like a rock.

If you want to take a look, first lubricate your calves well, because from the road the climb ascends steeply. Certainly if you want to be on site before sunrise, you'd better leave on time. Once at the top, you'll be treated to an unforgettable view over the Skye Peninsula. The peregrine falcon that breeds on the rocks here has chosen its spot very well.

INTO NATURE

The West Highland Way is Scotland's most popular **long-distance hiking trail**, and for good reason. You'll be walking through some of the iconic landscapes of the Scottish Highlands.

www.westhighlandway.org

Moving around Scotland's coastal region occasionally means taking a **boat**. Caledonian MacBrayne has been a loyal partner for many years.

www.calmac.co.uk

Wild camping is allowed everywhere. This principle is based on the old right of hospitality and is enshrined in the 'Scottish Outdoor Access Code'.

www.outdooraccess-scotland.scot

Looking for the most beautiful **nature reserves**? They're neatly bundled for you.

www.nnr.scot

The Scottish **autumn** is a highly colourful period with a constant flow of changes. Autumnal forests, mushrooms and golden yellow landscapes set the tone for a wonderful time full of photographic opportunities.

One of the most attractive **driving routes** is the North Coast 500. This takes you to several scenic locations along the northern coast of Scotland.

www.northcoast500.com

The world-famous but irritating midges can spoil the fun, especially in the summer months. And yes, there are lots of them! From late spring, the first specimens will buzz your way. Unfortunately, there are no effective means against these minuscule villains, but in the coastal areas the wind often provides a mosquito-free respite. This also includes the breeding bird island of Handa, off the west coast of Sutherland. Midges are hardly to be found there, seabirds all the more. Every spring thousands of animals visit this island to breed. This special place is an internationally important reserve for birds like auks, guillemots and great skuas. If you've had it with these noisy rascals, you can also scan the

surrounding sea for a while. Large marine mammals can often be discovered in the rich waters around this island: minke whale, bottlenose dolphin and other dolphin species frequently pass through, and with a bit of luck you'll catch a school of killer whales putting in an occasional appearance. A party, without midges!

HOTSPOTS

Achmelvich Beach
58°10'24.4"N 5°18'13.6"W

On this enclosed beach in a small bay you can imagine yourself on a tropical island. From the top of the surrounding cliffs you can enjoy a beautiful panorama.

Ullapool
57°54'02.7"N 5°09'39.3"W

The quaint town of Ullapool is located on Loch Broom. It forms a well-known base for trips to the Scottish Highlands and to the nearby islands.

Outer Hebrides
57°36'58.3"N 7°16'18.3"W

On a clear day you can see them from the mainland. The islands are at their best especially in spring, when the grasslands smell of flowers ('mahair'). This archipelago is also known for its corncrake population.

Bealach na Ba
57°25'01.9"N 5°42'23.7"W

Bealach na Ba is a winding mountain pass on the Applecross Peninsula. There you can imagine yourself at the end of the world. The road features huge changes in altitude, with views of the Isle of Skye the whole way.

Saint Kilda
57°48'45.1"N 8°34'16.7"W

The crossing to this uninhabited island is one of the most overwhelming day trips you can make in Scotland. An hour-long boat ride takes you to some of the highest cliffs in Europe. Scenically unique and home to many endangered seabirds. This archipelago is included in the World Heritage List.

HEIDELAND

THE NETHERLANDS

LASCIVIOUS DEER AND SYMPATHETIC GOOD GUYS

The heathland par excellence. That's how you can label the Netherlands. A large part of the country may be just about at sea level, but in the east of the Netherlands you can cycle till your trousers wear thin. No place for wide polders; in this surprising part of the Netherlands, the view is defined by steep push moraines covered with fragrant heaths and a patchwork of old forests. Every neighbouring country looks somewhat enviously at this remote and spacious corner of the world, where you can enjoy, endlessly and undisturbed, a solid chunk of top-quality nature, joined now and then by a herd of sheep or a group of chunky Galloways. These sympathetic good guys graze happily all year round and keep the heathland in top shape.

I'm still not sure what the best period is to roam the heath. In August, when the blooming heather is fragrant and buzzing, you won't know where to feast your eyes first. Not many weeks later, the urge to rut is everywhere. Then the lascivious red deer 'troat' or bellow like crazy, making a great show in their attempt to impress the females. You can experience it from the front row in the Veluwe, *the* heath arena par excellence. In winter, rare snow days turn the heath landscape into a tranquil fairy tale scene, just after the colourful forests have given the best of themselves. As a photographer or nature lover it's easy to enjoy yourself in 'heathland' for most of the year. The decisions are yours. Success assured!

FEATURED

For many artists, nature lovers and tourists, the purple heath has for many years been the pinnacle of what the Netherlands has to offer in terms of nature, with scenery to effortlessly captivate any visitor.

It really pays to get out early, before sunrise. Especially on windless mornings in spring and autumn, you are usually treated to extremely atmospheric conditions with low-hanging wisps of mist over the fens and the heath. Along the banks of the fens, dragonflies hang photogenically covered with glittering dewdrops. The colours in the landscape are phenomenal, you can die for the morning scent of the wet grasses and sandy soils. All that, with a bit of luck, to the musical accompaniment of a late-flying nightjar. Get up early is the message! Bet you'll return home with some fine pictures?

Even though the heath landscape appears devoid of any traces of human intervention, it was in fact created by the grazing and felling of the original forest. Chunks of the forest that managed to escape this process gradually developed into the most enchanting woodlands of the Low Countries, with often delightful names like Twickelerbos or the Onzalige Bossen with its straight, majestic beech avenues. And what about the Speulder- en Sprielderbos, perhaps the masterpiece of the Veluwe, where old oaks and beech trees have twisted themselves into impossible curves. The forest swings like nowhere else and the artfully streamlined tree trunks seem to move with the allure of an accomplished dance company. No surprise that many photogenic spots also exist here for the taking.

INTO NATURE

An interesting nature activity or excursion often starts or ends at a **visitor centre** in or on the edge of many heathland areas.
www.zoovaria.nl/uit-in-de-natuur/visitorscentra

Observation points always give you a different view of an area. Observation points and watchtowers are ubiquitous in the Netherlands, including in various heathland areas. There are many of them in the Veluwe.
https://weekendtoerist.nl/mooie-uitzichtpunten-op-de-veluwe

Cycling through the heath is a joy. An attractive **cycling network** has been skilfully layered over the landscape.
www.hollandcyclingroutes.com

Of course you can't ignore the late summer when the heather blooms. For hikers and photographers, this is the perfect time to indulge themselves. The peak of the **heather bloom** varies from year to year, but generally falls around the end of August.
www.visitveluwe.nl/artikelen/hier-geniet-je-van-de-bloeiende-heide

Natuurmonumenten manages a large portion of the Netherlands' heathlands. Who knows better than this organization's rangers where the best places are? They have listed the **most attractive heath routes** for you.
www.natuurmonumenten.nl/heideroutes

HOTSPOTS

Herikhuizerveld

52°01'39.2"N 6°01'25.1"E

By Dutch standards, the Veluwezoom is very rich in relief. Nowhere else in the Veluwe you can enjoy such panoramic views. The centrally located and hilly Herikhuizerveld is surrounded by the Beekhuizenseweg, embracing this area like a long panoramic route.

Planken Wambuis

52°04'15.4"N 5°44'18.6"E

Here you can walk and cycle endlessly through a beautiful landscape. You'll find the De Valenberg observation point to the northwest of the nature reserve.

Onzalige Bossen

52°02'29.4"N 6°01'49.3"E

De Onzalige Bossen is the name of an ancient forest area in the Veluwezoom National Park. The hilly forest is intersected by majestic beech avenues, including the dead-straight Koningslaan.

Kootwijkerzand

52°10'12.0"N 5°45'42.3"E

The 'Sahara of the Low Countries' is characterized by sand dunes and heaths with beautiful wild pines. The Kootwijkerzand is the largest active sand drift in Western Europe. From the De Zandloper observation tower you have a magnificent view.

Deelerwoud

52°04'52.0"N 5°53'50.7"E

In the Deelerwoud you'll find everything that makes the Veluwe attractive: large forests and endless heaths in a rolling landscape. If you want to avoid too many people, this area is a good alternative to the Hoge Veluwe.

Speulder- en Sprielderbos

52°15'08.8"N 5°39'31.1"E

One of the oldest forests in the Netherlands. Crooked oaks and beech trees characterize the area, popularly referred to as the 'forest of the dancing trees'.

While heathland may have a 'dry' image for many, it is quite the opposite. Heathland, forest, drifting dunes and fens alternate to lure a startling collection of wildlife: round-leaved sundew, silver-studded blue butterflies, tree pipit, saddle-backed bush cricket, banded darter dragonfly, smooth snake, nightjar, lizards... The long list seems endless.

And then it's spring and the activity erupts. Also for the rare moor frog it's time to gather again in some remote fen. During their search for mates, the males turn sky blue colour in a real metamorphosis and you can hear their choruses. Most migratory animals are observed in March with a peak in the second half of the month. If you walk on the heath during

this period, you'll undoubtedly hear the typical sound of this beautiful amphibian species.

FINNMARK
NORWAY

SUBARCTIC BIRDLIFE AND DESOLATE COASTLINES

To the far north of Scandinavia by car? For many, downright madness, and maybe I have to agree with them. Still, as a slow traveller, I enjoy every kilometre of the drive towards the Arctic Circle. You take the traffic jam around Hamburg and the queue to embark in Denmark in your stride, in the happy knowledge that in one day's time you'll be driving through grandiose landscapes that become more and more impressive as the kilometres clock up. The prospects too are highly attractive: killer whales, king eider ducks, otters, dizzying cliffs full of seabirds or perhaps a stray Arctic fox. I can already picture it all as my favourite Sonic Youth song reverberates through the speakers for the fifth time.

But stay focused. Dreamland is abruptly ended by a group of turkeys unabashedly courting in the middle of the road. What a spectacle, what posers too, those capercaillies.

It's now midnight, and the low-hanging sun casts a golden glow over the increasingly barren landscape. Welcome to Scandinavia, the adventure has now really begun!

I've been on the road for a week when I cross the border into Norway from Utsjoki, the somewhat desolate northernmost village in Finland. For the coming weeks, Finnmark, which includes the Varanger peninsula in the far east, will be my breathtaking playground. I've gradually exchanged the day for the sunny nightlife, the memory cards are full in no time. I'm stuck to this crazy place full of subarctic birdlife and phenomenal coastlines. It won't get any better!

You've only seen Scandinavia when you've crossed the mythical Arctic Circle. The landscape, nature and climate are of a different order. Distances between the often marginal-looking villages increase, people become more withdrawn. Come back in a few years' time, no pebble will seem to have been moved, the stockfish will still be drying in the constant wind. Nothing changes.

The Sami and their culture too are unique. They form the oldest ethnic group in this region. In Finnmark, most of them live in fishing communities near the Varangerfjord and the Tana River. Reindeer sheperds use the vast fjells as grazing grounds for their animals. The great famine of 1866 also forced many Finns towards the Norwegian coast, where they quickly learned to fish to survive. These Finnish immigrants

are called Kven, a term also used for the language they speak, a Northern Finnish dialect laced with Norwegian words, a language still spoken in a few small hamlets on the Varanger Peninsula.

To all nature freaks: good news! Watching or photographing wildlife in Finnmark is possible almost everywhere, the animals are often not shy at all. Living in no man's land, they're unaware of danger. The number of species in the Arctic area, with the exception of the coastal region, is generally low, but each species simply makes you fall off your chair. There's a black-throated diver bobbing on every pond in the interior or a nervous red-necked phalarope is twirling around like crazy.

The Finnmark coastline seems never-ending. Foxes and otters roam the stony beaches searching for goodies, even reindeer take an occasional walk there, noses in the wind, away from all the mosquito violence a little further inland.

A quick look out at sea will yield a handful of attractive finds. The Arctic tern, for example, of Arctic origin and of a graceful beauty. A genuine polar traveller. No living creature sees so much daylight per year. After a short breeding period in the far north, the bird migrates south for the winter, some even reaching the edge of the South Polar pack ice. Screaming loudly and often in groups, they scour the Arctic waters in search of food. They hang praying above the water surface before diving onto their prey. A divine sight!

INTO NATURE

From Belgium it's a three-days non-stop drive to the far north of Norway. But allow yourself some extra time to enjoy all the beauty along the way. From the south you reach Norway via a bridge that takes you from Denmark to Sweden, from where you drive on to Norway. You can also travel by **boat** from various departure points in Denmark or Germany.
www.aferry.com

There's no one **best travel period**; this very much depends on your objectives. If you're looking for birds, then it's fine almost all year round, with late spring/early summer (late May to mid-July) being the best time when all the breeding birds have arrived. Winter offers a completely different picture, in terms of both landscape and species.
www.visitnorway.com

Camping in Scandinavia is fantastic. Here allemannsretten (literally 'everyman's right (of access)') enables you to enjoy the great outdoors. You can set up your tent anywhere you want, as long as you stay away from cultivated and private land, and above all treat nature with respect.
www.visitnorway.com/plan-your-trip/travel-tips-a-z/right-of-access

In the **summer** you enjoy 24 hours of light. This can upset your biorhythm, especially if you lack the discipline to give yourself a break every now and then. In the **winter** the breathtaking northern lights are a bonus.

A traditionally expensive destination like Lapland doesn't have to leave you penniless. It's possible to travel the area **on a budget** with well-maintained, simple accommodation as a base, enabling everyone to discover the world at prices they can afford.
https://beyondborders.be

FEATURED

It's 3 a.m. The midnight sun casts an enchanting light on the cliffs of the breeding bird island of Hornøya, a five-star bird paradise in the Varangerfjord, brim full with a spectacular crowd of seabirds screaming their lungs out. You have to be here for the most attractive seabird phenomenon: the puffin, although you'll undoubtedly encounter other beautiful birdlife.

After two days and nights of incessant shooting, my body tells me it's time for a break and my respect for the thousands of sea-birds only increases. They fly non-stop back and forth to feed their young; where in heaven's name do they get all that energy from? That fish from the Barentsz Sea, that must be strong stuff! A long dirt path leads me through the frenzied mass of thousands of chattering birds to the lighthouse. There I can spend the night, in the company of these noisy cliff dwellers. Whether I'll get any sleep remains to be seen.

HOTSPOTS

Hornøya
70°23'15.3"N 31°09'17.6"E

Don't miss out on this legendary bird island off Vardø. It's every ornithologist's mecca.

Hamningberg
70°32'35.8"N 30°36'35.7"E

The 'End of Europe' sign that you may spot as you enter this hamlet needs no further explanation. Your journey stops here, and the only way forward is in your dinghy into the Barentsz Sea. You can spend hours on the desolate beaches in the area, searching for marine mammals and strolling among the washed-up Russian driftwood.

Nesseby
70°08'41.5"N 28°51'38.2"E

A mythical church in a blissful setting. Built in 1858 and the proud survivor of World War II. You can picnic with the white-tailed eagles flying around your ears. Also keep an eye on the pool behind the church, you'll always spot something nice.

Ekkerøy
70°04'14.4"N 30°07'38.2"E

Every year some 40,000 (!) black-legged kittiwakes come to breed on the imposing cliffs of Ekkerøy. From spring onwards you'll be overwhelmed by the constant screaming and completely immersed in the happy bustle of these criss-cross flying acrobats.

Ytre Syltefjord
70°34'32.5"N 30°15'27.5"E

A little more difficult to reach, but well worth an adventurous hike. The largest colony of northern gannets on the Varanger peninsula is found here, far from civilization.

Makkaur Lighthouse
70°42'26.3"N 30°04'43.6"E

This attractive lighthouse is located in Båtsfjord. The only access is by boat or on foot. And that's exactly what makes this place so exceptional. Alone in the world with the Barentsz Sea at your feet.

Turnstone — 240

Grey seal — 240

Arctic tern — 241

Atlantic puffin — 244

European brown bear — 6

Snake's head fritillary — 33

Black-headed gull — 36

Tengmalm's owl — 96

European brown bear — 113

Grey seal — 140

Great reed warbler — 155

Little owl — 189

Black-legged kittiwake — 242

See more of the photographer:
   www.wouterpattyn.com

Follow the photographer:
   www.facebook.com/wouterpattynphotographer
   www.instagram.com/wouterpattynphotographer
   www.linkedin.com/in/wouterpattyn
   www.vero.co/wouterpattynphotographer

Other work by Wouter Pattyn at Lannoo Publishers:
   The Image of Nature, How to catch light and life (2011)
   Natuur vanuit de hemel - De mooiste natuurgebieden van Vlaanderen in vogelvlucht (2014)
   Adembenemend België, verrassende natuur - Op stap in de mooiste natuurgebieden van België (2015)

Comments on the book are welcome at
   info@wouterpattyn.com

www.lannoo.com

Register on our website and we will regularly send you a newsletter with information about new books and interesting, exclusive offers.

Photography	Wouter Pattyn
Text	Wouter Pattyn
English translation	Michael Lomax
Design	Keppie & Keppie

If you have observations or questions,
please contact our editorial office:
redactielifestyle@lannoo.com

© Wouter Pattyn & Lannoo Publishers, Tielt, 2022
D/2022/45/456 – NUR 410
ISBN 978 94 014 8768 9

All rights reserved. Nothing from this publication may be copied, stored in an automated database and/or be made public in any form or in any way, either electronic, mechanical or in any other manner without the prior written consent of the publisher.